LET'S TALK ABOUT
INTERRUPTING

By Joy Berry

Illustrated by John Costanza

CHILDRENS PRESS ®

CHICAGO

Let's talk about INTERRUPTING.

3

You are INTERRUPTING when you
do something that makes
it difficult for other
people to think.

You are INTERRUPTING when you
do something that causes
other people to stop
what they are doing.

7

You are INTERRUPTING when you
talk when other
people are talking.

When someone interrupts you,
how do you feel?
what do you think?
what do you do?

11

When someone interrupts you,
   you may feel
   frustrated and angry;
   you may think the person
   is not fun to be with;
   you may decide to stay away
   from the person.

13

It is important to treat people
the way you want to be treated.

If you do not want people to
interrupt you,
you must not interrupt them.

15

Do not interrupt people who are
thinking or trying to do something.

Do not talk to them.

Do not make noises
that would bother them.

Do not do things
that would distract them.

Do not interrupt people who are talking to you.

Allow them to finish talking before you speak.

Say, "Excuse me," if you must interrupt them.

Do not interrupt people who are
talking to each other.

Do not talk with them
or listen to them
unless they ask you to.

Do not put yourself between
people who are talking
to each other.

Say, "Excuse me,"
if you must interrupt them.

21

Do not interrupt people who are talking on the telephone.

Do not talk to them.

Do not make it difficult for them to hear.

Do not make it difficult for them to think about what they are doing.

Do not interrupt people who are listening to something or watching TV.

Do not talk to them.

Do not make noise that makes it difficult for them to hear.

Do not change channels on the TV unless they want you to.

Do not put yourself between them and the TV.

Do not interrupt people who are
watching a movie or a performance.

Take your seat quickly and quietly.

Do not talk or make disturbing noises.

Eat neatly and quietly
if food is permitted.

Do not hit or kick the
seats around you.

Stay seated until
the movie or
performance ends.

27

Do not interrupt people who are resting or sleeping.

Stay away from them.
Be as quiet as you can.

29

To be happy, treat others
the way you want to be treated.

Everyone is happier
when no one is interrupting.

About the Author

Joy Berry is the author of more than 150 self-help books for children. She has advanced degrees and credentials in both education and human development and specializes in working with children from birth to twelve years of age. Joy is the founder of the Institute of Living Skills. She is the mother of a son, Christopher, and a daughter, Lisa.